Beats

to the

Punch

A Collection of Limericks
By Kevin Lucas

Beats To The Punch

A Collection of Limericks

Kevin Lucas

with photographs by
Terri Lucas

Grey Wolfe Publishing, LLC
PO Box 1088
Birmingham, Michigan 48009
www.GreyWolfePublishing.com

© 2013 Kevin Lucas
© 2013 Photographs by Terri Lucas
Published by Grey Wolfe Publishing, LLC
www.GreyWolfePublishing.com
All Rights Reserved

FIRST EDITION ISBN: 978-1-62828-008-1
SECOND EDITION ISBN: 978-1-62828-157-6
Library of Congress Control Number: 2013946355

Dedication

For Terri

Acknowledgements

This book would not have been possible were it not for the inspiration of one man, Chris Strolin, editor-in-chief at oedilf.com. His vision stirred, and continues to stir, my creative juices to a degree never seen before. I would like to thank him and the many workshop editors who have helped me fine-tune my limericks. Thanks also goes to my father. Many years ago following my college graduation and my revelation that I wanted to be a writer, he imparted these wise words to me: "Writers write every day." It took a while to sink in, but I think I've finally gotten the hang of it.

Attraction

You Said It!

Asked a gay, "See that guy? He looks great!"
Said his like-minded friend, "No debate!
Yes, indeed! I agree!
You got *that* right. I see,
Though, he's kissing a woman. Damn! Straight!"

College Studies

I love this well-rounded academy.
If my folks only knew, they'd think bad o' me.
My schoolwork's been lax —
I'm engrossed to the max
In the study of female anatomy.

Bigmouth

A bigmouth, devoid of discretion,
Not only revealed in confession,
But she blabbed in the pews.
Now we all know the news:
Father Vic is her carnal obsession.

Cafeteria Style

I choose, cafeteria style,
To date women with looks that beguile.
Choice of dishes is vast,
So I'll pass 'em by fast
If they're planning to walk down the aisle.

From Shy Guy To Sky Guy

When a man tried to speak to a hottie,
His stomach would always get knotty.
The guy found his voice
When he died; he'd no choice —
All around, a celestial body.

Babe Magnet

The thing that a woman expects
From a babe magnet, frankly, is sex.
But she also must know
There are likely, in tow,
Several women who want to be next.

She's Just Shy

I asked if she wanted to dance
In the hope it might lead to romance.
"Gotta run," she replied
As she swept me aside.
With that brush-off, she spurned my advance.

Beats To The Punch

Cities and Towns

Boom Towns

The profits from mines would entrance
Labor forces and more to the dance,
Making boom towns of old;
But deposits ran cold,
And they stood not a ghost of a chance.

Deadsville

Asked an out-of-town visitor, Hoyt,
"Where's the night life?" I told him, "Detroit
Is a relative deadsville,
'Cause not many heads fill
Downtown; there's not much to exploit."

Ill Noise

A Chicago lad, fart wunderkind,
Has town leaders profoundly chagrined
That a trend will appear.
Then their city, they fear,
Will be known for the wrong kind of wind.

Low Town

We've got high unemployment and crime,
And we're fat and illiterate. I'm
From Detroit. Our notorious
Ranking's inglorious.
Proudly we stood at one time.

Clothes

Clothes-Dryer

Through a rotating drum, heated air
Will evaporate moisture. It's rare,
After clothes-dryer tumbling,
To find me not grumbling
'Cause one of my socks lost its pair.

Alteration Needed

An alterer works on my clothes.
I'll have to lose weight, I suppose.
She said, "Letting out
Any more is in doubt.
I'm afraid that's as far as it goes."

The Old West Villain

There's the black hat; he enters a bar.
On his shirt, sheriff's stolen bronze star.
In his hand, .44.
If you want to know more,
We'll be back, so just stay where you are.

Proper Dress Code

Shirt-tail out, sleeves unbuttoned — that's rude.
Being carelessly clad will preclude
You from staying. The rest
Are quite properly dressed
For their nudist camp visit — they're nude.

Consumerism

Bottom Falls Out

A bikini store mannequin said,
"I'm embarrassed 'cause business is dead.
Drastic price drops — we got 'em.
What's more, since the bottom
Fell out, my face blushes bright red."

Marketing Tricks

Product pushers will often employ
Certain tricks: I sought perfume and, oy,
The ninth Beethoven played.
The last movement I made
Was to purchase the scent Eau de Joy.

Closing Time

Closing time is the time of the day
When a business sends patrons away.
But with patrons too few,
Then its days may be too.
A "For Rent" sign may be the display.

Dollar Days

I look at the dime stores that went
By the wayside and how much we spent
When compared to today.
It's a crime! What we pay
Has inflated 900 percent.

Centsless

There once was a five-and-dime shopper
Who hollered, "My money! Please stop her!
That lady just stole,
From my handbag, a roll
Full of pennies! I'm calling a copper!"

Creatures

Clingfish

Very small are these fish that can cling
Onto seaweed, rocks, any old thing
In the ocean. I waded
And almost invaded
Two clingfish caught up in a fling.

Donkey Exhibit

An exhibit where donkeys amass
Is on view to the public through glass.
One day at this zoo
A blind donkey broke through
And encountered a pane in the ass.

Black Widow

The long-legged daddy espied her
And wondered if he could excite her.
The black widow frowned,
"Don't be hanging around.
You'll regret that I'm just a one-nighter."

Debugging

"An ingredient used in this spray
Makes mosquitoes and gnats stay away,
So our barbecue guests
Won't be bothered by pests."
(Spoke too soon.) "Your mom's coming today?"

Crime and the Courts

Obtuse Jury

Both Darden and Clark had a goal —
Systematically blowing a hole
In the Simpson defense,
But the jury, quite dense,
Freed the killer of Ron and Nicole.

Just My Luck

To my first wife came bodily harm,
And my second, alas, bought the farm.
Will my luck turn around?
There's a pen pal I found
From my cell. Maybe third time's a charm.

The Wrong Crowd

Teaching right from what's wrong, we would mold.
Now our daughter is sixteen years old,
And my wife and I sigh.
The wrong crowd caught her eye;
We can't wait till our baby's paroled.

Diminished Capacity

My defense for that murderous crime
Was diminished capacity. I'm
Only serving two years,
'Cause a jury of peers
Bought the claim I was nuts at the time.

Thrill Kill

He found shooting his parents endorphin-
Releasing. In court, he's now morphin'
From happy to sad.
He's got chutzpah, that lad.
"Please take pity," he says. "I'm an orphan."

Freedom?

Long time serving, I'm wrinkled and wizened.
There's a slight chance I'll soon be disprisoned.
Oh, please! Is it time
To be freed for my crime?
The parole board, alas, says it isn'd.

Can It!

Can't you see that I'm trying to work?
Shut your piehole! You drive me berserk!
Your continuous yammer
Will get me the slammer,
For canning it *for* you, you jerk!

Bust Out

One who busts out of jail breaks the law.
Bust out laughing? That means you guffaw.
If a woman enhances
Her chest, then the chances
Are good she'll bust out of her bra.

The Wrong Suspect

"Hey, unhand me!" exclaimed a poor sap.
"You've confused me with some other chap.
So stop giving me grief.
I'm no butt blanket thief.
I'm not guilty; this here's a bum rap."

Dead To Rights

You were caught dead to rights — in the act
Of committing a crime; that's a fact.
You have nothing to say
To explain it away.
Better hope that the jury is stacked.

Craquelure

The shrinking of varnish attacks
Older artwork, producing fine cracks;
This is known as craquelure.
For art to look truer,
Smart forgers add cracks, which theirs lacks.

Death

Warm Body, Cold Sentiment

The body's still warm; can't you wait
Maybe two or three days to berate?
It's bad form — your assaults
And your listing of faults
On the day the poor guy meets his fate.

At Least I'm Not That Guy

Warned a farmer without a right arm,
"Get too close, you're inviting great harm.
Over yonder, a guy,
Not as careful as I,
Met a wood-chipping fate — bought the farm."

Desperation

His patience, endurance, and hope
Had been spent; he could no longer cope.
As a desperate plea,
He prayed, "God, set me free!"
And was found at the end of his rope.

My Comedic Legacy

My jokes will outlive this mere mortal.
Don't cry when I pass through death's portal.
When remembering me,
Snort and chuckle with glee.
What an honor if people would chortle!

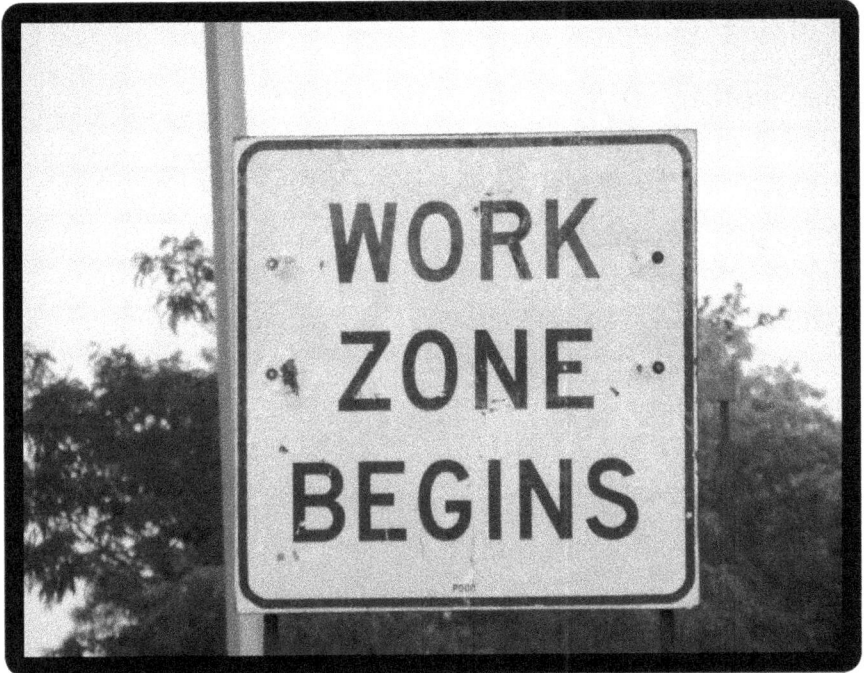

Employment and Unemployment

The Clock Watcher

Excessive attention I pay
To the clock, and I'm filled with dismay.
Just like watching a pot
Never boiling, I've got
A long wait till the end of the day.

Retirement Blues

I had worked 50 years. Now I'm through
With that life when my Mondays were blue.
But I'll make a confession:
I miss that depression,
'Cause now I don't know what to do.

The Brown-Noser

The boss's approval I seek,
So I brown-nose each day of the week.
Even weekends, I ask,
"Could I help with a task?"
"No. Stop fawning," his brilliant critique.

The Workweek Blues

My job sucks, and no weekday's a fun day.
I dream of retirement one day.
The weekend's sublime,
But too short. Then it's time
To go back to the salt mines on Monday.

Work (If You Want To Call It That)

I worked for a boss who was pushy,
So I looked for a job that was cushy.
My new boss, understanding,
Is far from demanding.
I netsurf all day on my tushy.

Plan B

An architect, not in accord
With the client (a vision ignored),
Said, "The failure is mine,
So I must redesign.
I'll go back to the old drawing board."

Shipping Out

Water vessels, I once had a hand in
Constructing; but leaving them standin'
Before they were done
Was a habit. "Last one,"
Said the boss. "No more ships you'll abandon."

The Weakest Link

"A chain is as strong as its link
That is weakest," the boss said. "You stink."
The business had slid
From the damage I did.
I got canned, and it's now in the pink.

Office Dalliances

My time-wasting dalliance annoyed
My stern boss; office girls I enjoyed.
But my playful flirtations,
Against regulations,
Is why I'm no longer employed.

High praise

In achieving the goals we've desired,
You've used cunning and craft; that's admired.
You're an artful, sly guy,
Which is why, with your eye
On my job, I must tell you, "You're fired."

Family

QUIET!

Life at *our* house is far from serene,
'Cause my kids make a riotous scene.
Every day, I try curbing
These uproars disturbing,
But bedlam's the normal routine.

Lead By Example

Remember, a good parent leads
By example. When planting those seeds,
Know your words are diluted
If not deeply rooted;
What's said must be backed up by deeds.

Dad's Christmas Gift

My dad says my intellect's dim,
That I'm foolish and act on a whim,
That I'm crack-brained and mad.
Last Christmas, for dad?
I gave a thesaurus to him.

Blood Is Thicker Than Water

Blood is thicker than water, they say,
Meaning family connections outweigh
And are stronger than those
Of outsiders. It shows
In that relative bond — DNA.

Finances and The Economy

Adjustable Rate Mortgage

My mortgage, adjustable rate,
Linked to indices (health of the state),
Shows there once was a time
When the lending was prime.
Now I watch as my assets deflate.

Consumer Confidence

When consumers have confidence high,
Then the likelihood's good that they'll buy.
But our current condition,
With jobs in remission,
Makes doubtful recovery's nigh.

Playing Terribly

When I play the piano, it shocks.
I'm so horrid, the keys should have locks.
It's the same when I'm playing
The market. I'm saying
I blow *Chopsticks* and blow blue chip stocks.

Lending And Borrowing

Banks had mandates to lend people money.
We were living the life; days were sunny.
But with no way to pay
It all back, now we say,
"Could we borrow some milk and some honey?"

Bottom Line

I was thinking my finances fine
Till my broker jumped in: "Bottom line?
What's the gist? What's the crux?
Your net income? It sucks.
I'd hold off on your plan to resign."

A Losing Investment

My stock market venture was lame,
And no winnings, alas, could I claim.
Turkey futures I tried,
But success was denied;
I could not get ahead of the game.

Big-Time Trader

The Wall Street exec knew his craft.
His firm's earnings were upwardly graphed.
Trouble came, unforeseen,
When the markets turned lean,
And this big swinging dick got the shaft.

Food and Drink

Baker's Dozen

When the bakery countergirl said,
"Thirteen bagels you get. You want spread?"
I explained, "They're delicious,
But I'm superstitious,
So give me a dozen instead."

Acid Drops

Misguided — arresting the young
For acid drops placed on the tongue.
When the cops found out we
Didn't do LSD
But did lemony drops, we got sprung.

At The Deli Counter

I got cold cuts from deli trainees.
I could tell that they lacked expertise,
Cutting jagged salami,
Roast beef, and pastrami;
The worst part was cutting the cheese.

Cornball

Popcorn balls, with my girl, I would savor.
Ah, molasses or caramel — what flavor!
It was love at first bite,
But like ships in the night,
She soon passed on the cornball I gave her.

Chiliburgers

Chiliburgers are good, but bring grief.
It's that chili con carne; ground beef,
Onions, peppers, and beans
On my hamburger means
I'll be seeking some bathroom relief.

Crème Brûlée

I'm becoming increasingly flustered.
I've tried, but I can't cut the mustard.
Sugar tops crème brûlée —
I can brown that okay,
But I keep overcooking the custard.

Challah

For that flavorful white bread I pine.
Made with eggs, it's a favorite of mine.
It's a braided, rich treat,
Which the Jews often eat.
My God, challah is simply divine.

The barfly

There once was a barfly named Norm.
Every day was the same; true to form,
He would take to his stool
And drink beer. As a rule,
No one else's butt kept that stool warm.

Mugging At The Pub

The Brit sent back beer at the pub
And yelled, "Waiter, you've managed to flub!
This mug is a stein!
Is this Germany? *Nein*!
Bring a tankard, you ignorant schlub!"

Digestive Distress

To eat lots of food, she'd the urge.
Now of vomiting, she's on the verge.
Both behaviors, each day,
Can be summed up this way:
Binge-and-purge, binge-and-purge, binge-and-purge...

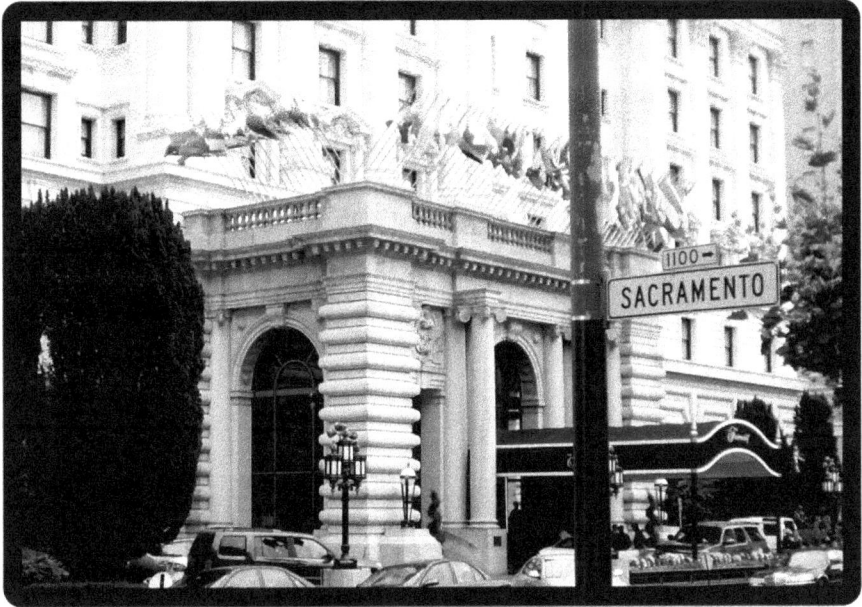

History

Boston Molasses Disaster

A disaster occurred up in Boston
(A street flood), which ended up costin'
Some lives — CO_2
Had built up, a tank blew,
And molasses some people got lost in.

Devil's Mark

The Devil's mark, branded on skin,
Is a sign she has Satan within.
Strip her down. Shave her hair.
There's a blemish right there.
Need more proof? Prick that witch with a pin.

Dead Man's Hand

The hand that Bill Hickok had held
Became legend when Jack McCall yelled,
"Take that!" — shot him dead
In the back of the head.
Before others could fold, Bill was felled.

Alcatraz

Come to Alcatraz Island, the Rock,
Via ferry; they daily will dock.
See a prison of old
And the cells, which would hold
Famous cons. Take a tour 'round the block.

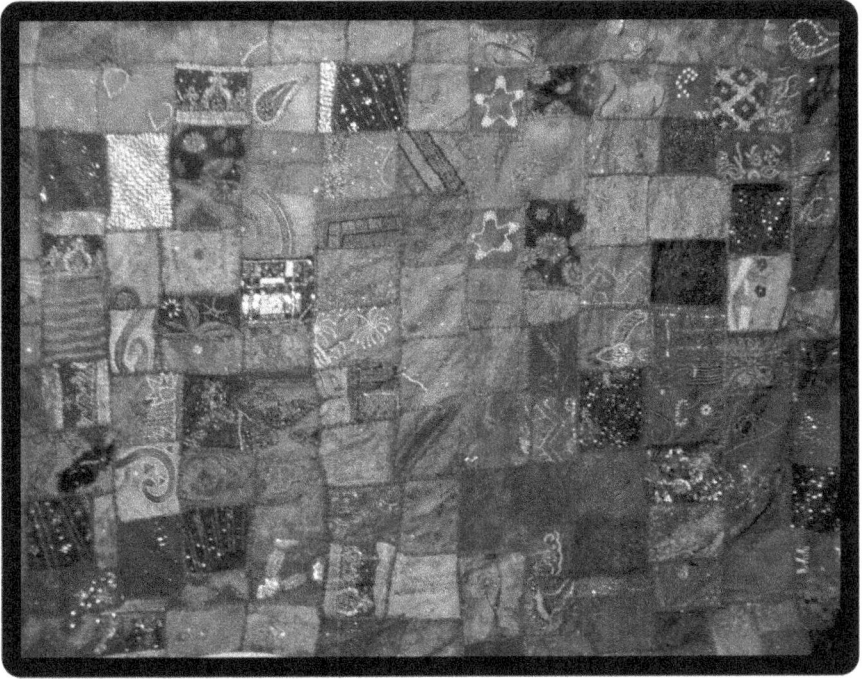

Hodgepodge

Major Achievement

I achieved what I set out to do.
All my schooling is finally through.
With my Liberal Arts major,
However, I wager
That good-paying prospects are few.

Frightful Fun

On amusement park rides I will go —
Not the ones that are sucky, oh no;
They blow chunks. I'm more merry
On rides that are scary
In spite of the chunks that I blow.

Black Friday

4 a.m. — she awakes. It's absurd.
She's still full on the holiday bird.
But Black Friday has deals
At the stores, which appeals
To my wife and the rest of the herd.

Dactylology

Dactylology's used by the deaf.
(Finger spelling, that's *d-e-a-f*.)
By the way, if the mood
Strikes for great finger food,
Go to Rollie's — thumbs up to their chef.

The Data Is In

I'm led, by the facts that I've viewed
And the analyzed stats, to conclude
That, if diets are fad,
The success rate is bad.
By proponents, such data's pooh-poohed.

That Time

"Hurry, mom!" she cried out. "Call a nurse!"
Twelve years old, she had felt nothing worse —
The cramps and the blood,
The emotional flood.
Then her mom said, "Don't fret. It's the curse."

Gran, You're A Trip

Said my acid freak grandmother, "Dearie,
Without LSD my life's dreary.
I can't get enough.
I got hooked on the stuff
After hearing a guru named Leary."

Brain Dump

My thoughts and my feelings I keep
In a blog. People say I'm not deep
In my brain dumps; I tend to,
By being a friend to
Insomniacs, put them to sleep.

Is Anybody Listening?

This notion can bring you to tears:
If you're talking and nobody hears.
If this happens to you,
Go to England (please do).
Find Prince Charles; he can help — he's all ears.

Blonde Moments

Blonde moments that used to be rare
Have increased since I colored my hair:
My gray matter's drained;
I've become scatterbrained;
But of fun, I've had more than my share.

Literature

Oedipus

Blindly, Oedipus did as was fated:
Killed his dad; with his mother, he mated.
On the latter, this lesson:
Before you go messin'
Around, know you two aren't related.

Summary Judgment

I read blurbs on the back. In the flaps,
I read summarized contents. Perhaps
If the book jacket's piquing
My interest, I'm seeking
The middle to fill in the gaps.

Brick Up

Said the third little pig, "You guys saw
What became of your sticks and your straw.
If you brick up the walls,
You'll be safe from the squalls
Like the ones from this wolf that we gnaw."

Penance

An author, notorious crook
In the past, urges folks, "Take a look
At my life — how I've turned
Things around and I've learned
That it's best to live life by the book."

Marriage

Remember When You...

Her memory for detail's a curse.
Now my marriage can't get any worse.
She'll precisely recall
Not one screw-up, but all.
Then she'll quote for me chapter and verse.

A Daisy A Day

In his mind, vivid images play
Of their lives ere his wife passed away,
Of the love gone unbroken,
Conveyed by a token —
He gives her a daisy a day.

Common Ground

"Our shared interests will not reappear,
Nor beliefs," said my wife with a tear
In her eye. "Common ground
Can no longer be found."
"Yes, the feeling is mutual, dear."

Brownie Points

A woman who's pleased by her spouse
In their sex life may nonetheless grouse.
Brownie points won't be earned
In the bedroom, I've learned.
They accrue if I help 'round the house.

Medical

Ear, Nose, And Throat

Said the doc when I went for a checkup,
"Take your clothes off." I thought, "What the heck?" Up
I stood to take leave.
(I'm not freakin' naïve.
ENTs only deal with the neck up.)

A Move To The Right

If your right lung collapses, you'll free
Up some space. (This has happened to me.)
Since my heart had a mission
For dextroposition,
I find now I vote GOP.

Doctor Visit

Today's visit reminds me I've one
Of the *worst* doctors under the sun.
There's pain on my right side.
"Well, look on the bright side,"
He says. "On your left, you have none."

Px For Disaster

Chirographical issues delay
Us from treatment. Our docs have a way
To make pharmacists shrug,
'Cause the scrip for the drug
Is illegible — what does that say?

Cyesis

"Hey doc, how much time have I got
With this case of cyesis — a lot?"
"You have eight months to go."
I was thinking, "Oh, no!"
Till he told me I'm having a tot.

Bloodletting

Theodoric? You're viewed with disdain.
Joan, the miller's wife, thinks you're insane,
As her daughter now pays
For your bloodletting ways.
There's no humor in draining a vein.

My Coma Dream

I awoke in my hospital bed
From a coma. The first thing I said:
"Though I dreamed the idea
Of Jerry Garcia,
I'm grateful I'm back from the dead."

Beats To The Punch

News

News Bias

Most reporters have liberal views,
And this bias comes through with the news.
All their "experts" and sources
Lean left, which of course is
Their goal — give us news that they choose.

Walter Cronkite

Watching *CBS News* — in the day it was
Tops in the ratings — folks say it was
Cronkite, the man
Who was anchor (not Dan),
Whom they trusted the most. That's the way it was.

Lobsters

"No challenging questions here, please.
Pave my road to the White House with ease."
And so who do we thank?
All the press in the tank
Who, with softballs, made winning a breeze.

He's Our Man!

What charisma! I'm backing Barack.
On the White House, he'll sure have a lock.
A case open and shut —
His election. So what
If I'm part of the media flock?

Politics

The Press Secretary

"Beyond question, your question is dumb —
No disputing — as dumb as they come..."
(Tough questions deflected —
An art I've perfected)
"...On that issue, the President's mum."

Cycle Of Dependency

The underclass stuck in the slums
Are beholden to Washington bums
Who keep handing out scraps.
This behavior entraps
And perpetuates living off crumbs.

Financial Meltdown

We'd a whole lot of folks taking naps;
The result was the Wall Street collapse.
Now we're stuck with the bill,
Which is nearly a tril.
We share blame; we elect the same saps.

Absolute Power

My support for our leader turned sour
When I learned of his absolute power;
It corrupts absolutely.
I now am astutely
Aware and in need of a shower.

The Election Of 1912

Bull Moosers were Teddy supporters
Who resented the delegate hoarders
Who made Taft nominee
Of a split GOP,
Giving Wilson some new living quarters.

Jump On The Bandwagon

His campaign's mass appeal had me wowed,
And I wanted to follow the crowd.
I decided to jump
On the bandwagon. "Chump"
I'm now calling myself; I'm not proud.

Antimarket

Those who live in a Communist land
Know that choices aren't many at hand.
Antimarket's the course
That their leaders endorse.
I'm so glad we're not buying that brand.

Disgracing The Office

His shenanigans happen too often,
And support has continued to soften.
Will another report
(The unflattering sort)
Be the ultimate nail in his coffin?

Baptism By Fire

The onslaught of issues is draining.
He's baptized by fire — the training
Is scant for this guy;
He gets by on the fly.
Let's just hope there's some wisdom he's gaining.

JFK In Reverse

John F. Kennedy told us, "Ask not
What your country can do (dot, dot, dot)."
Now that notion's reversed.
A Big Government thirst
Has some ask, "How'd we get to this spot?"

Bipartisanship

I informed freshman Congressman Clem
That bipartisanship for a Dem
Isn't giving a little
To meet in the middle;
Instead it's agreeing with them.

The Election Of 2000

"Count the votes!" They were counted; Bush won.
"Well, then count 'em again! We're not done
Till the victor is Gore."
The Supremes said, "No more."
Cries of "Stolen!" had only begun.

Clean Break

I will implement policies fast
'Cause we need a clean break from the past.
What has been status quo,
For eight years, now must go.
With my blueprint, the future's recast.

Working Together

"All for one, one for all" — it would seem
All of Congress had worked as a team.
Pet projects were banned.
Kumbaya gripped the land.
But, alas, it was only a dream.

Tell Them What They Want To Hear

The candidate talked a good game.
Now he's prez, and his tenure is lame.
Seems his promises vowed
Were just words to the crowd.
He's all talk and no action — a shame.

The Stimulus

Massive federal spending has failed
In the past when economies ailed.
A healing infusion
Of cash is illusion.
By fools who now lead, this plan's hailed.

Buy Into

You uncritically find him compelling.
Your ardent support is quite telling.
Go ahead and believe,
But, my friend, you're naive
To buy into that garbage he's selling.

Hale Or Ail?

Obama, Pelosi, and Reid
Will be breaking the bank, guaranteed.
Their concern for our health
Means depletion of wealth,
So much so that our grandkids will bleed.

John McCain

His words and his deeds disagree,
And the point is, my friends, you can see
That I've got a clear record;
My opponent's is checkered.
At the end of the day, vote for me.

Audacity

On audacity, daring and bold,
And his confident air, we were sold.
In the path he's now leading
Us down, there's no heeding
Restraint — we face wreckage untold.

Promise Land

Remember the promises spoken?
They're now only promises broken,
Like the tax cuts he swore —
He just chose to ignore.
Trust is shattered. What shit were we smokin'?

Winged Porkers

As soon as pigs fly I'll adapt
To a liberal agenda uncapped.
I'll adjust to that smell
On a cold day in Hell.
(Frickin' Dems are in power — I'm trapped!)

Committed

Committed, the nation's in sync
With our president's will. We all drink
From the Kool-Aid he's selling.
We find him compelling.
State-run media's great! Don't you think?

The Watergate Stoolie

In the book *All the President's Men*,
We meet Deep Throat, a man with a yen
To stay safely concealed
While misdeeds he revealed.
This led some to do time in the pen.

Between A Rock And A Hard Place

A rock and a hard place I faced.
Both these options were met with distaste.
I was voting between
A progressive (obscene)
And a socialist (bodily waste).

The Healthcare Bill

Said the Rep up on Capitol Hill,
"The thousand-plus page healthcare bill
Is reform that we need,
But it's too big to read,
Because reading it makes me quite ill."

Body Odor

On the body, bacteria grow
In the presence of sweat. You will know
By the odor that's there.
In the White House, the air
Is befouled by another B.O.

Business As Usual

It's business as usual — we send
To D.C. folks who promise to end
The corruption. They face,
Though, a system in place
That consumes them, then furthers the trend.

Relationships

Shutting You Out

The horrible things that you said to me,
Not to mention the lies that you fed to me,
Make me hate you so much.
The intensity's such
That I shun you completely; you're dead to me.

Distortion

What I told you — I couldn't be clearer.
But you twist what I say; you're a hearer
Of only a portion,
Creating distortion.
Your prism of truth? Fun house mirror.

Love Gone Sour

Between us is widening space,
Not the kind that you'd find in a race,
But aloofness, a **distance**.
I sense a resistance
To love; you no longer give chase.

Known Quantity

For years I've known Lucifer; though
He is far from ideal, he's my beau.
Unknown Damien tried,
But a date I denied
Because better the devil you know.

Concubine

You're my concubine, darling. Don't grouse.
Though your status is low in this house
And our children aren't heirs,
In our carnal affairs
You come first. Go downstairs; ask my spouse.

Dead Ringer

"You're unfaithful!" she screamed. "So we're through!"
I explained, "This dead ringer, so true
Was her likeness, I swore
When I kissed her she bore
An uncanny resemblance to you."

The Inevitable Breakup

Said a gay to his ex, "You're a great man,
But surely you knew it was fate, man.
We've talked of our dreams
To form comedy teams,
But neither one wants to play straight man."

Not a chance

"Billionth (point, then eight zeros, then one)
Of a chance," she remarked, "we'll have fun."
I had to destroy it —
"*You* needn't enjoy it,"
I said, dropping odds down to none.

Lesbos

Getting shipwrecked on Lesbos was Ben,
Who learned women there don't have a yen
For the straight life, and so
Having nowhere to go,
He accepted his fate to date men.

Yawn

"Can I see you again?" I asked Beth
At date's end. She said, "Don't hold your breath.
Truth be told, you're a loser,
An absolute snoozer,
A deadass who bores me to death."

There's More To It?

Said the girl I was dating (now ex),
"I want more, and you're not that complex.
You've not left adolescence.
Reduced to your essence,
All you really boil down to is sex."

It's Hopeless

Dating Jill was my plan; I commenced it,
But hopelessness hovered — I sensed it.
My efforts would stall;
She put up a brick wall,
And my head started banging against it.

Ouch!

For my good-looking ex, I still yearned,
But my love for her wasn't returned.
So I made it my aim
To forget my old flame,
Since I'd carried a torch and got burned.

Recycled

A man planned to marry my daughter.
He showed her the ring that he'd brought her.
She checked the inscription
And had a conniption.
His ex made them dead in the water.

Love's Illusion

That magician you're dating's a joke.
Don't you think that it's time you awoke?
His act, disappearing
A lot, has you hearing
Deception; he always blows smoke.

AC/DC

"AC/DC?" he asked of his date.
"Heavy metal," she said. "Yeah, they're great!"
When she learned what he'd meant
Was her sexual bent,
She said, "No. Take me home 'cause I'm straight."

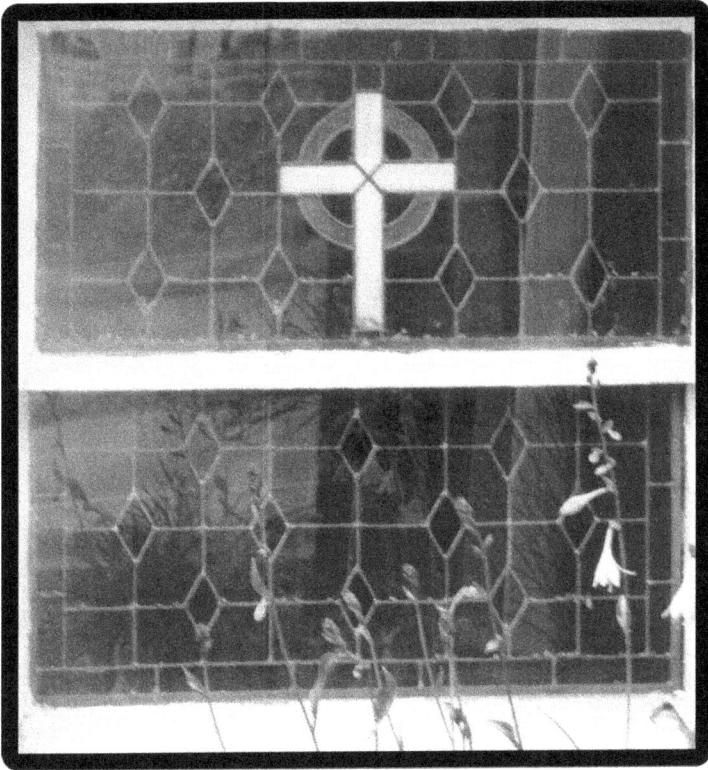

Religion

Blood Money

For blood money, Judas betrayed
Jesus Christ, but the coins he got paid
He would end up returning.
He hanged himself, learning
The treasonous part that he played.

Boxed In

Are you feeling boxed in and you yearn
To be free, but have nowhere to turn?
Here's a path unexplored:
Put your faith in the Lord;
He'll dispose of your weighty concern.

Christianity's Origin

"You can put me to death on the cross,
Though to crucify me is no loss,
But a gain," Jesus said.
"By all means, go ahead.
A religion will start, says the Boss."

The Good Samaritan

A man, stripped and beaten when found
By a trekker, was Jericho bound.
The robbers who fled
Adummim thought him dead.
Through God's grace, the man rose off the ground.

Revelation

"Armageddon!" the Witnesses drill
In my head. Now I've made myself ill
Over prophecies dire
That we all will expire.
Friends say, "Here's how to save yourself — chill."

Coincidence

Coincidence? Woman and man?
Accidentally's how we began?
Whereas you take the stance
We arose quite by chance,
I believe we were part of God's plan.

Salvation

This world hasn't known such behavior
So selfless as, Lord, when you gave your
Own life for our sins.
Our salvation begins
When we recognize you as our Savior.

Agnostic

I'm agnostic, i.e., noncommittal.
The concept of God is a riddle;
Same for heaven and hell.
Others' "truths" just don't jell.
I devoutly inhabit the middle.

The Body And Blood Of Christ

His body's symbolically bread,
And the wine stands for blood that He shed.
This communion is where
Fellow churchgoers share
His true spirit, on which we are fed.

Church Service

The church service lasted too long.
So assented the congregate throng.
Clearing throats led the pastor
To preach a bit faster
And reach the recessional song.

Creationism VS. Evolution

My rejection of God came about
Over time hearing people devout.
Evolution is lacking,
They say, yet they're backing
A theory that raises more doubt.

Black Magic

My mom says I'm going to Hell,
'Cause I chanted a black magic spell
For the purpose of evil —
Pandemic upheaval.
Does it count that I wished my mom well?

Buyer's Remorse

If God, the Creator of Earth,
Were to sell it today, He'd find mirth
In the buyer's remorse;
We've been drifting off course
For a long time and lessened its worth.

Jesus Freak

Said a born-again Christian, "I pray
To the Lord up above every day;
I've a personal bond..."
I jumped in to respond,
"If it's personal, keep it that way."

The Ills Are Alive And Well

"Society's ills never pass,"
Says our priest. "It's a constant morass."
His Sunday assault
Is to always find fault.
We all call it his critical mass.

Ash Wednesday

I reflect on my sins and repent
This Ash Wednesday, the first day of Lent.
With these ashes I trust
That I'm dust unto dust,
And this cross stands for Him who was sent.

Crucifix Fish

God created the crucifix fish
To be more than just food on a dish.
That its skeletal section —
A cross — brings reflection
Of Christ is His ultimate wish.

The Wheat And The Tares

The Wicked One works through bad seeds,
Which are placed among good. They're like weeds,
But when harvest arrives
And they learn who survives,
They'll regret that they did evil deeds.

Sow Good

God sees all. He'll repay us in kind
For our deeds, good or bad. Keep in mind
We shall reap as we sow.
Let good character show,
And His blessings in Heaven we'll find.

Christ Almighty

"Christ Almighty!" he'd shout, not to pray
To the Lord in a reverent way;
With this expletive, Dad
Made it clear he was mad.
We all knew things were far from okay.

What The Devil?

I went to a meeting of Wiccans,
And Satan was there. (The plot thickens.)
I asked for a light,
And he lit up the night
With his hellfire; it hurt like the dickens.

His Body

In the spirit of Christ, we're engrossed;
We partake of His body, the Host.
(It's like heavenly manna.)
No second banana,
JC is the most Holy Ghost.

God's Promise To Me

God spoke, and I thought it sublime.
He said, "Up from the gutter you'll climb..."
Then my glee turned to tears
When He said, "...30 years
Down the road, my son, all in due time."

Cain

"There's a reason your brother's not found,"
God tells Cain. "He cries out from the ground
That you killed him. Your fields
Will produce paltry yields,
And you'll restlessly wander around."

The Beginning

At the outset, He got underway
With His work, but not long did He stay.
Without breaking a sweat
In the dark, He said, "Let
There be light," and then called it a day.

Silence Is Golden

A young monk, gabby Lou, won't employ
Meditation; this tends to annoy.
The head monk dressed him down.
Contrite Lou, with a frown,
Cried, "Hey, abbot, I've been a bad boy!"

King Solomon's #1 Hit

There's a season to everything, so
Says the Bible. Pete Seeger, we owe
For adapting the words,
Adding music. The Byrds
Turned it into the hit we all know.

A Rich Inheritance

"The meek," said a biblical scholar,
"Shall inherit the earth in their squalor.
Jesus meant that the blessed
Aren't the money-obsessed.
Worship Him, not the almighty dollar."

Sayings

Baby Blues

Hormone levels have plunged; she's depressed.
She can't bond with her baby; she's stressed.
Tears and mood swings begin.
Baby blues have set in,
And she's craving a luxury — rest.

Daddy's Girl

My daughter's my ultimate fan.
She's a daddy's girl, sweet Lindsay Ann.
Don't know why, but she's fond
Of a tightly-knit bond
With her grateful and lucky old man.

Burning Bridges

Who we'll meet in this life, we don't know.
So speak kindly to friend and to foe.
The more bridges we burn,
The less grace in return;
Paths destroyed leave you nowhere to go.

Backhanded Compliments

"You look nice, almost unrecognizable."
"I envy your chest; mine's so sizable."
If no tact is your tack —
Making cracks with some back-
handed compliments — hushing's advisable.

About Face

We sang as we marched at high noon.
The place is our base, Camp Lejeune.
Sarge yelled, "Company, halt!
About face!" Without fault,
A one-eighty we did — changed our tune.

Break A Leg

Said my actor friend, "Don't wish me luck;
That's bad luck." So I said, "Hope you suck.
Break a leg. Why not two?
Get a bad stomach flu.
And I mean that sincerely, you schmuck."

Catch Ya On The Flip Side

"Please, an interview, ma'am?" "Yes, I'll letcha.
I'm busy right now, but I'll catch ya
On the flip side." "Okay.
I can wait one more day.
See you later, Ms. Palin." "You betcha!"

Calling Card

Every time we go walking, he'll pee
On some hydrants and many a tree.
So wherever we roam,
He will know the way home
By his calling card. "Dad, follow *me*!"

Cry Wolf

She cried wolf once too often; she conned
All the people who came to respond.
Thus, when *real* help was needed,
Her calls went unheeded.
Then God came to call from beyond.

Compassion Fatigue

A confessional priest, I would care
Way too much. Now compassion's not there,
'Cause fatigue has set in;
My concern has worn thin,
And I haven't the heart left to spare.

Bee In Your Bonnet

There's a bee in your bonnet; your head
Has a notion it can't put to bed.
Your obsession annoys.
Honey, no one enjoys
That you drone on and on. Enough said!

Big Cheese

Out in Monterey, Jack's a big cheese,
The head honcho of all VIPs.
He's the cream at the top,
The big wheel. Shall I stop
With this metaphor string? Just say please.

The Devil's Advocate

Devil's advocates challenge and make
A case counter for argument's sake.
It's a way to find flaws
While supporting a cause.
Don't believe the positions they take.

Blow The Whistle

If you know that an organization's
Unlawful, report violations.
Blow the whistle — reveal
What they try to conceal.
This may lead to extended vacations.

Camp It Up

I came out. I'm no longer a liar.
Now I'm camping it up. Some inquire
Of the swish in my walk,
And the lisp in my talk,
And my voice being two octaves higher.

Battle Of Wits

I studied the great funny Brits
For my upcoming battle of wits.
Someone told me, "No, no.
Study smart people." So
I gave up on Pythonian skits.

Bats In The Belfry

I'm known for my gross impropriety;
I flout all the norms of society.
They say that I've bats
In the belfry, and that's
Taking into account my sobriety.

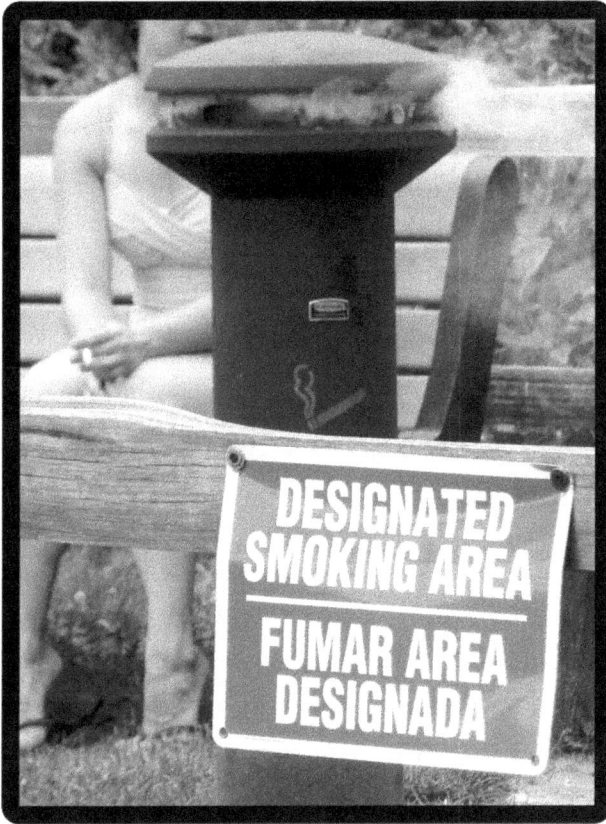

Smoking

Dhudheen

I take some tobacco and stuff
My dhudheen. Then I light up and puff
On this short-stemmed, clay pipe.
To my friends, though (the type
Who are dippers), I'm not up to snuff.

Thunder Strikes

Overcome by a bad bronchiolar
Disease was an avid young bowler.
The second-hand smoke
At the lanes made him croak.
Now an angel, he's one holy roller.

Breaking The Habit

I'll quit smoking today — I'm emphatic!
My spouse said, "You must be pragmatic.
Ditch those cigs that you store
In our house's top floor.
Until then, it's a nicotine attic."

Freedoms Under Fire

Some leaders, today antismoke,
May tomorrow attempt to revoke
Other freedoms they tag
To be vices — a drag.
It is high time the masses awoke!

Social Issues

Evolution

Darwin theorized man and ape linking.
Opposition, their "evidence" shrinking,
Says we're made from the sod
In the image of God.
Will they ever evolve in their thinking?

Darwin

"On Man's origin, light will be thrown."
So said Darwin (biologist), known
For his study of creatures
With similar features.
Minds closed, some refuse to be shown.

Bring It On!

Bring it on! We will never be cowed.
We'll stay standing resilient and proud.
Are we up for a fight
Against evil? Damn right!
Terror simply will *not* be allowed.

Consensus

"Scientific consensus," we're told,
But is junk science what we've been sold?
"Global warming's man-made" —
If you fail to be swayed,
Then you're bound to be left in the cold.

The Bush Doctrine

They attacked on American soil,
And you question my methods to foil
Any future attacks?
These are terrorist acts.
From tough measures we must not recoil.

Bellicosity

The factions expressed bellicosity
And started to fight with ferocity.
They say bitter ill will
Gave them reason to kill.
Where's it rooted? Ingrained animosity.

Big Brother

Big Brother's ubiquitous eyes
See us all through surveillance; its guise —
To nab crooks. But the cost
Is our privacy's lost
With our freedom; we watch their demise.

The Abortion Pill

The abortion pill purges what dwells
Early on in the womb. What compels
The right-to-life foes?
Here's the question I pose:
Are you *for* eighty-sixing those cells?

Legislating From The Bench

Democracy often is spurned
By some activist judges, concerned
We're a nation of fools
Where majority rules.
Thus, our will is, at will, overturned.

Beat Swords Into Plowshares

"Let's beat swords into plowshares. No more
Will our nations be training for war."
Now we've unforeseen woes,
'Cause we're plowing for those
Who signed peace pacts they chose to ignore.

Anti-Establishment

Son, the anti-establishment gist?
Power structures and mores are dissed.
Cut your grandpa some slack.
He grew up a while back
In the Sixties when many were pissed.

Back In *My Day*

A permissible attitude flows
Through society's veins, and it shows.
Today's toleration
Begets degradation.
Yes, nowadays anything goes.

Senate Armed Services Committee

"Mr. Rumsfeld, Iraq was no threat.
You were wrong." "Mr. Kennedy, let
Me inform you who's wrong.
What happened so long
Ago shows us just who is all wet."

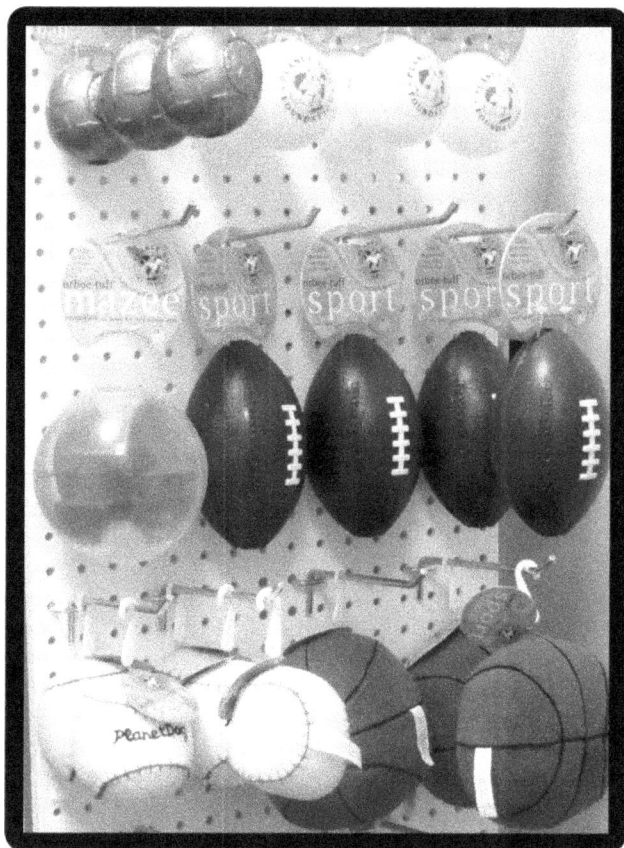

Sports

The Detroit Lions

They've had 50-plus years of futility.
They're lacking in bouncebackability.
Return to good form?
Good at sucking's the norm
On the football field. Oh, the humility!

Barn Burner

"This barn burner's really high-scoring!"
My friend yelled. "You're nuts for ignoring.
So close — both teams fighting
To win — it's exciting!"
No fan of the sport, I said, "Boring."

Rah! Rah! Rah!

She can cheerlead — the best that I've seen.
She's a jumping and dancing machine.
When she dates, out of step
Are the jocks, 'cause her pep
Is a 24/7 routine.

A Whopper!

My fish tale — I thought people bought
It all hook, line, and sinker. Distraught,
I came to find out
That they knew all about
My big lie; it was I who was caught.

Gridiron Great

The quarterback oft gave the ball
To the tailback, who, not one to fall,
Had the other teams frazzled
With moves that bedazzled.
This running back's now in the Hall.

The 2008 Super Bowl/David Versus Goliath

The Patriots, 18 and 0,
Were the favorites to win the big show.
With determined defiance,
The underdog Giants
Surprisingly conquered their foe.

Mark "The Bird" Fidrych

Flying high was The Bird, rookie year.
A hard landing abridged his career.
But we'll fondly recall
How he gave it his all
As he talked to the ball — a bit queer.

Transportation

Backseat Driver

"It's a wonder we still are alive.
Slowing down sure would help us arrive
Safely home," she critiqued.
Then I screamed, anger peaked,
"Either shut the hell up or *you* drive!"

No Off Switch

A collision I'd hoped to avoid,
But my wife, that damn airbag, annoyed
With her chatter nonstop.
With a vein 'bout to pop,
I then crashed, and the airbags deployed.

Car Windows

"You had hand-turned crank handles? Bizarre!"
Said my son. "Were they standard? Each car?"
"Power windows," I said,
"Arrived later, which led
To us grasping how lazy we are."

Road Construction

Traffic barrels determine our fate
For as long as they cause us to wait.
Appropriately,
People ceasing to be
At that time will be known as "the late...."

Car Mechanics

Make sure the mechanics you choose
Get consistently stellar reviews.
A blown gasket today,
Fixed a haphazard way,
Pissed me off, got me blowing a fuse.

My Piece Of Junk

This junker I'm driving is crappy.
Repairman, I beg, make it snappy.
My wedding's at stake,
And I don't want to make
A whole church full of people unhappy.

Mutual Departure

Her jalopy was gathering rust;
You could say she was also, and just
As her car ran its last,
The old woman had passed.
Her road ended; she'd bitten the dust.

Braking distance

I totaled the car. Goodness sakes!
I judged wrongly the distance it takes
Upon braking to stop —
Braking distance. Now Pop
Says I'm grounded for life. Them's the breaks.

Beats To The Punch

TV, Movies, Music and Fame

American Idol

I tried out for *American Idol*.
I just knew I could land me the title.
Simon spoke, spelling doom:
"You're aware, I presume,
That to sing well is utterly vital."

Cut To The Chase

Said poor Archie, who sensed just a trace
Of the point, "Can you cut to the chase?
Edith, tell me the core
Of your story, no more."
But she rambled all over the place.

Missing The Beat

We agreed to have Fonzie on drums.
Now we find out he's clumsy, but mum's
The word. Play it cool,
Because only a fool
Would be telling the Fonz he's all thumbs.

The Blues Brothers

Chicago police in their squad
Cars and Illinois nazis (how odd)
Pursued Elwood and Jake.
With some orphans at stake,
Elwood called it "a mission from God."

Die Hard

Bruce Willis, the actor who starred
In a series of films I regard,
Will save next, with his guns,
Senior-citizen nuns.
Working title: *Old Habits Die Hard*.

The Big Bopper

Not foreseeing the gold he would strike,
The Big Bopper stepped up to the mike
And, with voice loud and strong,
Set a phone call to song —
"Hello, BAAAby...you KNOOOW what I LIKE!"

Ageless

I was made to look back-in-the-day.
Now I'm worried what people will say.
With that "Photoshop" deal,
Fans will know it's not real
With my wrinkles all airbrushed away.

Existing On Celebrity

"Well, I'll be! As I live and breathe! Damn!
If it ain't Barbra Streisand! Uh, ma'am,
You were speeding, you know,"
Said a cop. "Is that so?"
Answered Babs. "Don't you know who I *am*?"

Bird In A Gilded Cage

The price of my fame? I'm a bird
In a gilded cage. Safe from the herd,
I'm confined where I dwell;
This huge mansion's my cell.
I'll be free when I'm dead and interred.

Fleeting Fame

With the public, some favor I'd curry,
But the spotlight brought just a brief flurry —
15 minutes of fame
When they all knew my name.
Lacking talent, I now start to worry.

Kevin Lucas

Kevin Lucas grew up in Northwest Detroit as the fourth of five children. At a young age, he developed an interest in words and became an avid Scrabble player and occasional writer. His favorite reading materials were reference books like dictionaries and thesauri. Kevin met his future wife, Terri, in 2000 and inherited her son, Adam, when they married in 2003. Their daughter, Lindsay, was born in 2004.

Beats To The Punch

www.ingramcontent.com/pod-product-compliance
Lightning Source LLC
Chambersburg PA
CBHW060817050426
42449CB00008B/1693